BENJAMIN FRANKLIN

AND THE DISCOVERY OF ELECTRICITY: SEPARATING FACT FROM FICTION

by Megan Cooley Peterson

CAPSTONE PRESS
a capstone imprint

Published by Capstone Press, an imprint of Capstone
1710 Roe Crest Drive, North Mankato, Minnesota 56003
capstonepub.com

Library of Congress Cataloging-in-Publication Data
is available on the Library of Congress website.
ISBN: 9781666339536 (library binding)
ISBN: 9781666339543 (paperback)
ISBN: 9781666339550 (eBook PDF)

Summary: In 1752, the sky in Philadelphia, Pennsylvania, darkened. A thunderstorm was coming. But Benjamin Franklin was ready with his kite and a key. What would his experiment show about the nature of lightning? And did it lead to the discovery of electricity? Discover what's fact and what's fiction in the legendary story about Ben Franklin's famous kite experiment.

Editorial Credits
Editor: Carrie Sheely; Designer: Bobbie Nuytten; Media Researcher: Donna Metcalf; Production Specialist: Whitney Schaefer

Image Credits
Alamy: North Wind Picture Archives, 15, Science History Images, 7, 13, 18, 26 (top left); Getty Images: Bettmann, 14, FPG, front cover (top left), H. Armstrong Roberts/ClassicStock, 28, Heritage Images, 22, ilbusca, 10, Science & Society Picture Library, 8, 27, Sepia Times/ Universal Images Group, 17, Universal History Archive, 21, 26 (bottom right), Universal Images Group, 25; Shutterstock: Everett Collection, 5, Fer Gregory, front cover (bottom), Morphart Creation, 9, Pau Buera, back cover (middle right), 11, vkilikov, front cover (top right)

Source Notes

Page 9, "blow" Timothy J. Jorgensen, "When Benjamin Franklin Shocked Himself While Attempting to Electrocute a Turkey," Smithsonian Magazine, November 22, 2021, https://www.smithsonianmag.com/history/when-benjamin-franklin-shocked-himself-while-attempting-to-electrocute-a-turkey-180979094/, Accessed February 2022.

Page 20, ". . . As soon as any . . . " Nancy Gupton, "Benjamin Franklin and the Kite Experiment," The Franklin Institute, June 12, 2017, https://www.fi.edu/benjamin-franklin/kite-key-experiment#:~:text=Despite%20a%20common%20misconception%2C%20Benjamin,worked%20extensively%20with%20static%20electricity, Accessed February 2022.

Printed and bound in the USA. PO#5195

Table of Contents

Words in **bold** are in the glossary.

Introduction

It was a stormy June day in Philadelphia in 1752. Most people stayed inside to avoid the rainy weather. But author, scientist, and inventor Benjamin Franklin had other plans. Many stories say he headed out into the gloomy afternoon with his young son, William, and a kite. A metal key dangled at the end of the kite string. As the kite flew into the dark sky, Franklin and his son waited. Suddenly, lightning struck the kite and lit up the key. Today, many people believe Franklin had just discovered **electricity**! But is that what really happened?

Benjamin Franklin's kite experiment has become one of the most famous legends of American history.

Many people know the story of Franklin and his kite. He made one of history's most important discoveries that day. Except the story isn't completely true. Electricity had been known for more than a thousand years. And Franklin wasn't even the first to experiment with it. So, what really happened when Franklin flew his kite?

Chapter One

Experimenting with Electricity

Benjamin Franklin's interest in electricity was sparked in the 1740s. People in Europe were familiar with **static electricity**. Experiments with glass tubes had been done for a long time. People rubbed glass rods against fabric. Then they touched the rods to objects and other people. The rods made a small shock.

Franklin's British friend Peter Collinson sent him a glass tube to do similar experiments. Franklin bought more tubes and put on shows at his house. Guests watched as he "drew sparks" from objects using **friction**. He made bells ring and toys move using tiny zaps of electricity. Franklin believed that all objects had electrical **charges**. These charges could move from object to object. Even clouds, he thought, held electrical charges that were released as lightning.

Scientist William Gilbert performed experiments with magnetism and static electricity in the 1500s.

HOW DOES STATIC ELECTRICITY WORK?

Static electricity is an electrical charge that sits on an object's surface. Most objects have a neutral charge. Rubbing two objects together can cause particles called **electrons** to jump from one object to the other. One object then has a negative charge. The other has a positive charge. This movement of electrons makes static electricity.

Leyden Jars

Pieter van Musschenbroek

Franklin stored static electricity in a Leyden jar. Dutch scientist Pieter van Musschenbroek invented the jar in the 1740s. The Leyden jar was made of glass and filled partway with water. A cork closed the top of the jar. A wire or nail pierced the cork and dipped into the water. When static electricity touched the exposed wire or nail, it flowed into the jar and was stored there.

At the time, scientists thought the charges were stored in the jar's water. Franklin discovered that the glass itself held the charge, not the water. In 1748, he created his own storage system using 11 panes of glass. He named it a battery.

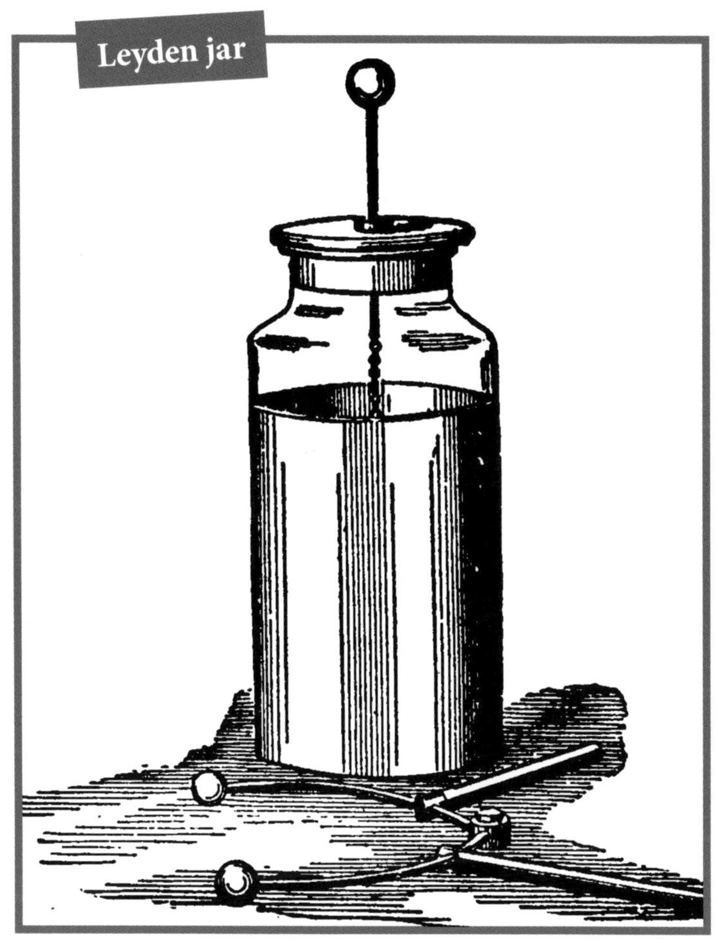

A DANGEROUS DEMONSTRATION

During one demonstration in 1750, Franklin accidentally touched the Leyden jar wire. His guests reported a bright flash and a snap as loud as gunfire. Franklin felt a "blow" travel through his entire body. His hand turned white and went numb for a short time.

Learning More

Franklin didn't use electricity only to entertain people. He also tried to learn more about it. In one experiment, Franklin electrified a glass jar. He held a sharp needle near the glass. A spark jumped to the needle. A blunt object had to be held much closer to draw a spark. He found that pointed objects drew sparks more easily.

Ben Franklin did several experiments to learn about the properties of electricity.

In 1749, Franklin read news reports about homes, trees, and churches damaged by lightning. He saw that lightning and electricity had a lot in common. They both gave light and moved quickly. They also made a loud cracking noise. Franklin began to wonder: Was lightning electricity? Could he create a tool to protect people and buildings from lightning strikes? He needed to design an experiment to find out.

Lightning bolts strike Earth about 3 billion times per year.

Fact!

Franklin coined the term "electrician" to describe people who experimented with electricity.

The Sentry Box Experiment

Franklin wanted to prove that lightning was electricity. But the kite experiment wasn't his first choice. In July 1750, he designed the sentry box experiment. His idea was to put a pointed iron rod on a tall building. The rod would stick down through the roof like the wire in a Leyden jar.

Someone would sit inside the building as the "sentry." This person would hold a wire attached to the bottom of the rod. The rod would gather an electric charge from the clouds during a storm. The charge would then travel down the rod and through the wire. The sentry would be able to feel the charge. To avoid a deadly shock, the sentry would sit on an **insulated** surface and hold the wire with a wax handle.

Franklin believed the sentry box would help show that lightning was a form of electricity.

Success in Europe

Franklin wrote about his idea in several letters to his friend Peter Collinson. In 1751, Collinson published the letters as a book. It was a huge success in Europe. In May 1752, Thomas François Dalibard in France successfully carried out Franklin's sentry box idea. A few days later, another French scientist repeated it. At that time, it took weeks for mail to arrive in the American colonies from Europe. Franklin was unaware that his idea had succeeded.

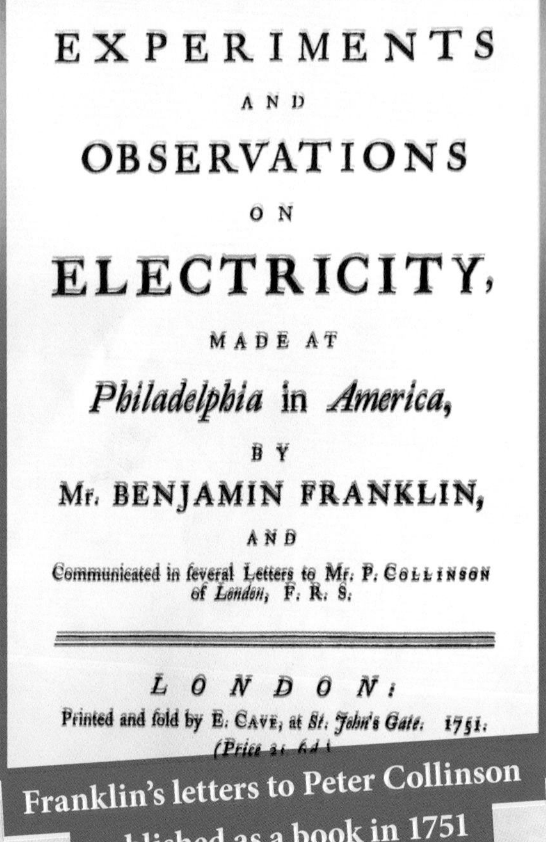

EXPERIMENTS

AND

OBSERVATIONS

ON

ELECTRICITY,

MADE AT

Philadelphia in *America*,

BY

Mr. BENJAMIN FRANKLIN,

AND

Communicated in ſeveral Letters to Mr. P. COLLINSON of *London*, F. R. S.

LONDON:

Printed and ſold by E. CAVE, at *St. John's Gate*. 1751.

(Price 2s. 6d.)

Franklin's letters to Peter Collinson published as a book in 1751

In 1752, at least two French scientists proved that Franklin's sentry box idea could work.

Franklin wanted to try his sentry box on top of a church being built in Philadelphia. But construction on the church was slow. Franklin didn't want to wait. He had to come up with another way to test his **theory** about lightning.

Chapter Two

Flying a Kite

Benjamin Franklin decided to test his ideas with a kite. He built the kite out of cedar wood and silk cloth. At the top of the kite, he placed a wire that was 12 inches (30 centimeters) long. He believed the wire would gather a charge like the rod in his sentry box idea. A piece of twine hung from the bottom of the kite. It was tied to a piece of ribbon. A key dangled from the spot where the twine and ribbon met.

Franklin and his son went to a small shed on a windy afternoon in June 1752. Franklin needed the ribbon to stay dry to avoid a shock. He stood just inside the shed. William helped get the kite into the air. Then they waited.

Instead of an iron rod, Franklin tested his ideas about lightning with a kite, a key, and some wire.

When sparks jumped from the key to his hand, Franklin knew there was an electric charge.

Soon, dark storm clouds passed overhead. At first, nothing happened. Then Franklin noticed small strands of the twine begin to stand straight up. When he moved his knuckle to the key, he received a shock.

Suddenly the rain started, which got the kite and twine wet. Electricity moves more easily through water and wet objects. Even more sparks jumped from the key to Franklin's hand. His experiment had worked! The metal wire was pulling electricity from the clouds down to the key. He had shown that lightning was electricity.

Fact!

It's true that Franklin flew the kite with his son William. But William was 21 years old at the time, not a small boy.

Chapter Three

What Really Happened

One big **myth** about Franklin's experiment is that a bolt of lightning hit his kite. If that had happened, Franklin would have been killed on the spot.

He later wrote about the experiment for the newspaper he owned, the *Pennsylvania Gazette*. Franklin wrote, " . . . As soon as any of the Thunder Clouds come over the Kite, the pointed Wire will draw the Electric Fire from them."

Historians agree that lightning didn't hit the kite. The "fire" was simply electrical charges from the storm. A bolt of lightning striking Franklin's kite is an exciting story. But it's not true.

Another myth about Franklin is that he discovered electricity. But people had observed static electricity long before he was born. Greek philosopher Thales first wrote about it around 600 BCE. He noted that rubbing **amber** against animal fur would cause dust to "stick" to it. In 1600, British scientist William Gilbert came up with a word for this attraction. He called it *electricus.* In the early 1700s, Stephen Gray discovered that electric charges passed easily through **conductors** such as metal.

In 1729, British scientist Stephen Gray discovered that electricity could travel through conductive materials such as wire.

Is it possible Franklin never flew his kite at all? William never wrote about or spoke of the experiment. Franklin didn't write about it until October 1752. His short *Gazette* report gave instructions on how to carry out the experiment. But he didn't give any personal details about what happened. Some historians say this proves Franklin never completed the experiment. They think it was only an idea.

In 1767, Dr. Joseph Priestly wrote a book about the history of electricity. One part was about Franklin's experiment. Franklin gave Priestly a firsthand account about it. It was Priestly who said the experiment happened in June 1752.

Dr. Joseph Priestly

Most historians agree that Franklin respected science. If he said the experiment succeeded, that was likely true. However, Franklin often let time pass before talking about his experiments with others. This may explain why many details of what really happened have changed over time.

Franklin briefly mentioned the kite experiment in his 1788 autobiography. He said he was happy it had been successful. But he gave no other details.

Chapter Four

The Legacy of Franklin's Experiment

Franklin wanted to use his new knowledge about lightning to help people. He went back to experimenting with sharp and dull objects. He knew that sharp objects gathered charges more easily. He wondered if a pointed metal rod on top of a building could save the building from lightning strikes.

Franklin studied the way lightning passed through buildings. He noted that lightning passed easily through metal and caused little damage. But if lightning struck wood or plaster, it could cause a fire.

In the summer of 1752, Franklin put rods on the Pennsylvania State House and the Pennsylvania Academy. A brass wire attached to the rod would carry the electricity safely into the ground. These were the world's first lightning rods.

A Philadelphia man named William West was one of the first to praise Franklin's invention. He had a lightning rod on his house. When a bolt of lightning struck it, the charge went safely through the wire into the ground. West checked his home for damage and found none.

When West checked the lightning rod, he found that the tip of it had melted.

Early Franklin lightning rod, 1752

In September 1752, Franklin climbed onto his roof and attached a 9-foot- (2.7-meter-) long lightning rod. A wire ran down from the rod through a glass tube in the roof. The wire continued to his bedroom door, where it was split in two. Franklin hung a bell at the end of each wire. Then he hung a small brass ball with a silk thread between the bells. The bells would ring whenever the rod gathered charges from clouds. The tinkling bells probably delighted Franklin.

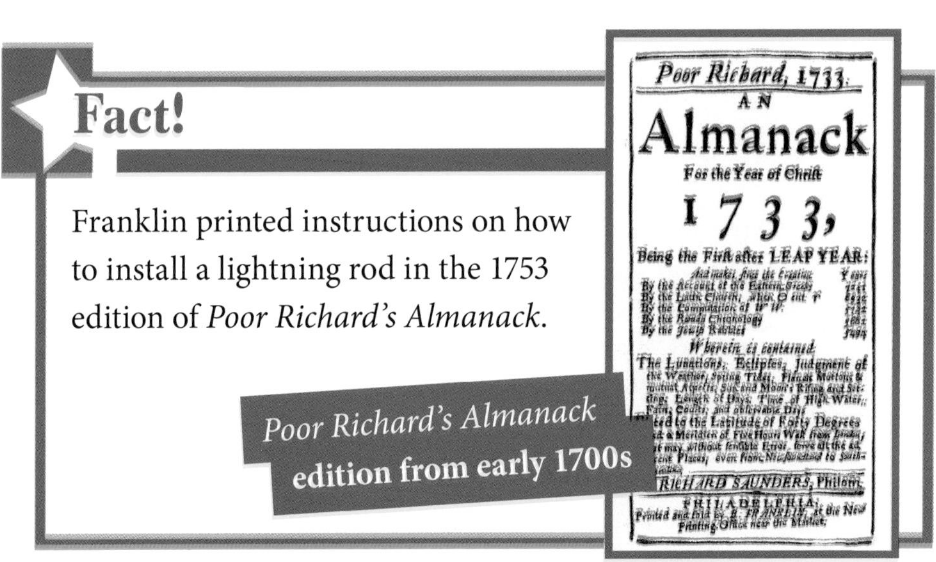

Poor Richard, 1733.

AN

Almanack

For the Year of Christ

1733,

Being the First after LEAP YEAR:

Wherein is contained

The Lunations, Eclipses, Judgment of the Weather, Spring Tides, Planets Motions & mutual Aspects, Sun and Moon's Rising and Setting, Length of Days, Time of High Water, Fairs, Courts, and observable Days.

RICHARD SAUNDERS, Philom.

PHILADELPHIA:

Printed and sold by B. FRANKLIN, at the New Printing-Office near the Market.

Fact!

Franklin printed instructions on how to install a lightning rod in the 1753 edition of *Poor Richard's Almanack*.

Poor Richard's Almanack edition from early 1700s

BIFOCALS

As Franklin grew older, his eyesight got worse. He needed two pairs of glasses. He used one pair to see things from a distance and one for objects up close. He got tired of switching between glasses. So he combined the lenses into one! These were the first bifocal glasses. Today, many people still wear bifocals.

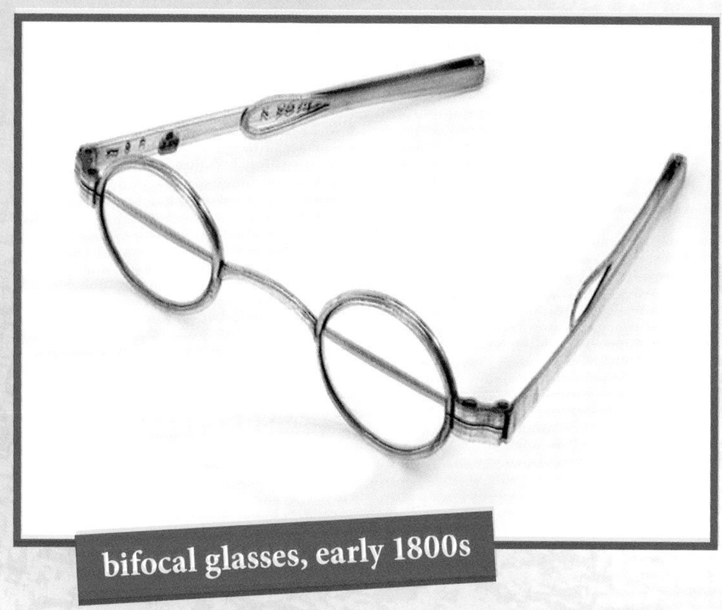

bifocal glasses, early 1800s

More than Just a Kite

When Franklin flew his kite in 1752, he proved that lightning is made of electricity. He also invented the lightning rod, which many people still use today. His invention has saved many lives and buildings.

Franklin's work with electricity made him famous. When the American colonists went to war with Great Britain in 1775, Franklin was asked to sail to France. His fame helped him convince France to join the colonists in their fight for independence.

painting of Benjamin Franklin, 1785

Benjamin Franklin flew a kite in a thunderstorm and changed the world. His inventions and scientific experiments are still studied today.

Fact!

Franklin signed both the Declaration of Independence and the U.S. Constitution.

The Mythology of Benjamin Franklin and the Discovery of Electricity

Fiction Benjamin Franklin discovered electricity.

Fact Greek philosopher Thales first wrote about static electricity in 600 BCE. Many other scientists studied it before Franklin.

Fiction Franklin's kite was struck by lightning.

Fact Franklin's kite picked up electrical charges from the storm, not a lightning strike.

Fiction Franklin's son William was a young boy when he helped fly the kite.

Fact William was 21 years old at the time of the experiment.

Fiction Benjamin Franklin was the first to prove lightning is electricity.

Fact French scientist Thomas François Dalibard was the first to show that lightning is electricity when he completed Franklin's sentry box experiment in 1752.

Glossary

amber (AM-buhr)—a yellow-brown substance formed from fossilized tree sap

charge (CHARJ)—an amount of electricity running through something

conductor (kuhn-DUHK-tuhr)—a material that lets heat, electricity, or sound travel easily through it

electricity (ih-lek-TRIH-suh-tee)—the movement of electrons that can be used to make light and heat or to make machines work

electron (i-LEK-tron)—a tiny negative particle in an atom that travels around the nucleus

friction (FRIK-shuhn)—the resistance caused by one surface moving over another surface

insulated (IN-suh-lay-tuhd)—protected from electric shock by materials that block the flow of electricity

myth (MITH)—a false idea that many people believe

static electricity (STAH-tik i-lek-TRIH-suh-tee)—the buildup of an electrical charge on the surface of an object

theory (THEE-ur-ee)—an idea that explains something that is unknown

Read More

Dickmann, Nancy. *Benjamin Franklin: The Man Behind the Lightning Rod*. North Mankato, MN: Capstone, 2020.

Proudfit, Benjamin. *Benjamin Franklin and the Lightning Rod*. New York: Gareth Stevens Publishing, 2023.

Shulman, Mark. *Benjamin Franklin: Inventor of the Nation!* San Diego, CA: Portable Press, 2020.

Internet Sites

Benjamin Franklin House: Ben Franklin's Lightning Rod
benjaminfranklinhouse.org/event/virtual-class-ben-franklins-lightning-rod/

The Franklin Institute: Benjamin Franklin
fi.edu/benjamin-franklin/resources

Time for Kids: Benjamin Franklin
timeforkids.com/g34/benjamin-franklin/

Index

About the Author

Megan Cooley Peterson is a children's book author and editor. Her book *How To Build Hair-Raising Haunted Houses* (Capstone Press, 2011) was selected as a Book of Note by the TriState Young Adult Review Committee. When not writing, Megan enjoys movies, books, and all things Halloween. She lives in Minnesota with her husband and daughter.